Bric-a-Brac Qui

This scrappy-looking quilt is really made with a roll of 35 different 2½"-wide strips.

PROJECT SPECIFICATIONS

Skill Level: Beginner
Quilt Size: 56" x 72"
Block Size: 8" x 8"
Number of Blocks: 35

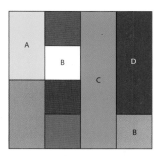

Bric-a-Brac
8" x 8" Block
Make 35

FABRIC Measurements based on 42" usable fabric width.	#STRIPS & PIECES	CUT
35—2½" x 42" strips light, medium and dark prints	70	4½" A pieces
	175	2½" B squares
	35	8½" C pieces
	35	6½" D pieces
1 yard black mottled	2	2½" x 40½" E
	3	2½" x 42" F
	7	2¼" x 42" binding
1¼ yards blue print	6	6½" x 42" G/H
Backing		62" x 78"

SUPPLIES

- Batting 62" x 78"
- Neutral color all-purpose thread
- Quilting thread
- Basic sewing tools and supplies

COMPLETING THE BLOCKS

1. To complete one Bric-a-Brac block, select two A, five B and one each C and D pieces, all in different colors.

2. Join two A pieces on the short ends to make an A unit as shown in Figure 1; press seam in one direction.

Figure 1

3. Join four B squares to make a B unit, again referring to Figure 1; press seams in one direction.

4. Sew B to D to complete a B-D unit, again referring to Figure 1; press seam toward D.

5. Arrange and join the pieced units with C to complete one Bric-a-Brac block referring to the block drawing; press seams in one direction.

6. Repeat steps 1–5 to complete 35 Bric-a-Brac blocks.

Completing the Quilt

1. Arrange and join five Bric-a-Brac blocks to make a row as shown in Figure 2; press seams in one direction.

Make 7

Figure 2

2. Repeat step 1 to make seven rows, pressing seams in adjacent rows in opposite directions.

3. Arrange and join the rows, alternating the placement of the pressed seams, to complete the pieced top; press seams in one direction.

4. Sew the E strips to the top and bottom of the pieced center; press seams toward E strips.

5. Join the F strips on short ends to make one long strip; press seams open. Subcut strip into two 60½" F strips.

6. Sew an F strip to opposite long sides of the pieced center; press seams toward F strips.

7. Join the G/H strips on short ends to make one long strip; press seams open. Subcut strip into two 44½" G strips and two 72½" H strips.

8. Sew G strips to the top and bottom and H strips to opposite long sides to complete the pieced center; press seams toward G and H strips.

9. Sandwich the batting between the completed top and prepared backing; pin or baste layers together to hold.

10. Quilt as desired by hand or machine; remove pins or basting. Trim excess backing and batting even with quilt top.

11. Join binding strips on short ends to make one long strip. Fold the strip in half along length with wrong sides together; press.

12. Sew binding to quilt edges, mitering corners and overlapping ends. Fold binding to the back side and stitch in place to finish. ■

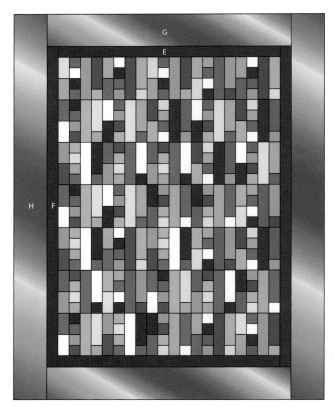

Bric-a-Brac Quilt
Placement Diagram 56" x 72"

Road Block

Two strip-pieced blocks make up the design in this quilt made with Jelly Roll strips.

PROJECT SPECIFICATIONS

Skill Level: Beginner
Quilt Size: 64" x 76"
Block Size: 6" x 12"
Number of Blocks: 40

Road Block 1
6" x 12" Block
Make 20

Road Block 2
6" x 12" Block
Make 20

FABRIC Measurements based on 42" usable fabric width.	#STRIPS & PIECES	CUT
44—2½" x 42" assorted navy, deep red, green and tan strips sorted into 22 darks and 22 lights	40 40	6½" light C pieces 6½" dark D pieces
⅝ yard dark green tonal	6	2½" x 42" E/F
2 yards deep red print	7 7	6½" x 42" G 2¼" x 42" binding
Backing		70" x 82"

SUPPLIES

• Batting 70" x 82"
• Neutral color all-purpose thread
• Quilting thread
• Basic sewing tools and supplies

COMPLETING THE BLOCKS

1. Label the remaining 2½"-wide strips as light (A) and dark (B).

2. Sew a B strip between two A strips with right sides together along the length; press seams toward the B strip. Repeat to make five A-B-A strip sets.

3. Subcut the A-B-A strip sets into 20 (8½") A-B-A units as shown in Figure 1.

Figure 1

4. Sew D to the top and bottom of each A-B-A unit to complete 20 Road Block 1 blocks referring to the block drawing; press seams toward D.

5. Sew an A strip between two B strips with right sides together along the length; press seams toward the B strips. Repeat to make five strip sets.

6. Subcut the B-A-B strip sets into 20 (8½") B-A-B units as shown in Figure 2.

Figure 2

7. Sew C to the top and bottom of each B-A-B unit to complete 20 Road Block 2 blocks referring to the block drawing; press seams toward C.

Completing the Quilt

1. Join four each Road Block 1 and Road Block 2 blocks to make a row as shown in Figure 3; press seams toward Road Block 2 blocks. Repeat to make five rows.

Make 5

Figure 3

2. Join the rows, turning every other row, referring to the Placement Diagram for positioning; press seams in one direction.

3. Join the E/F strips on short ends to make one long strip; press seams open. Subcut strip into two 60½" E strips and two 52½" F strips.

4. Sew E strips to opposite long sides and F strips to the top and bottom of the pieced center; press seams toward E and F strips.

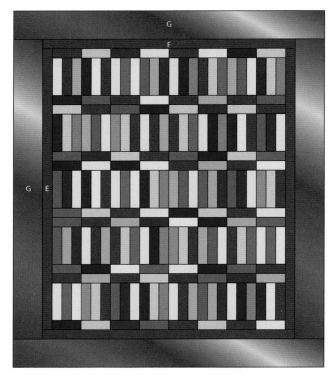

Road Block
Placement Diagram 64" x 76"

5. Join the G strips on short ends to make one long strip; press seams open. Subcut strip into four 64½" G strips.

6. Sew a G strip to opposite long sides and then to the top and bottom of the pieced center to complete the pieced top; press seams toward G strips.

7. Sandwich the batting between the completed top and prepared backing; pin or baste layers together to hold.

8. Quilt as desired by hand or machine; remove pins or basting. Trim excess backing and batting even with quilt top.

9. Join binding strips on short ends to make one long strip. Fold the strip in half along length with wrong sides together; press.

10. Sew binding to quilt edges, mitering corners and overlapping ends. Fold binding to the back side and stitch in place to finish. ■

Cross Ties Throw

One block design, two value variations and precut fabric strips make this quilt super-easy to make.

PROJECT SPECIFICATIONS

Skill Level: Beginner
Quilt Size: 56" x 66"
Block Size: 10" x 10"
Number of Blocks: 20

FABRIC Measurements based on 42" usable fabric width.	#STRIPS & PIECES	CUT
10—2½" x 42" strips light prints or tonals	4 4	2½" C squares each strip 4½" E pieces each strip
10—2½" x 42" strips light prints or tonals	1 2 2	10½" F piece each strip 6½" G pieces each strip 2½" I squares each strip
10—2½" x 42" strips dark prints or tonals	1 2 2	10½" A piece each strip 6½" B pieces each strip 2½" D squares each strip
10—2½" x 42" strips dark prints or tonals	4 4	2½" H squares each strip 4½" J pieces each strip
½ yard light blue print	5	2½" x 42" K/L strips
1¾ yards yellow print	6 7	6½" x 42" M/N strips 2¼" x 42" binding
Backing		62" x 72"

SUPPLIES

- Batting 62" x 72"
- Neutral color all-purpose thread
- Quilting thread
- Basic sewing tools and supplies

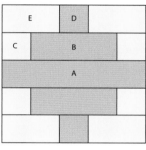

Cross Ties 1
10" x 10" Block
Make 10

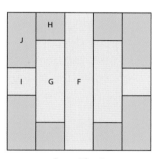

Cross Ties 2
10" x 10" Block
Make 10

COMPLETING THE BLOCKS

1. To make one Cross Ties 1 block, sew C to each end of B; press seams toward B. Repeat to make two B-C units.

2. Join two E pieces with D to make a D-E unit; press seams toward D. Repeat to make two D-E units.

3. Arrange and join the pieced units in rows with A as shown in Figure 1 to complete one Cross Ties 1 block; press seams toward A. Repeat to make 10 blocks.

Figure 1

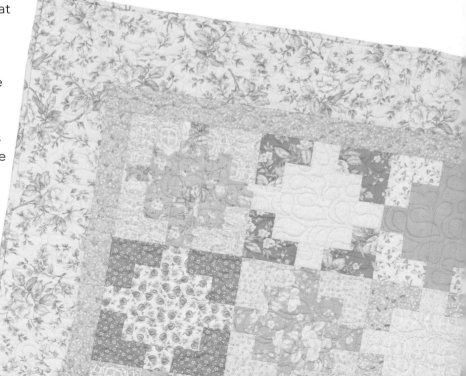

4. Repeat step 1 with G and H to make two G-H units; press seams toward H.

5. Repeat step 2 with I and J to make two I-J units; press seams toward J.

6. Arrange and join the pieced units with F as shown in Figure 2 to complete one Cross Ties 2 block; press seams toward F.

Figure 2

7. Repeat steps 4–6 to make 10 Cross Ties 2 blocks.

Completing the Quilt

1. Join two each Cross Ties 1 and Cross Ties 2 blocks to make a row as shown in Figure 3; press seams toward Cross Ties 2 blocks. Repeat to make five rows.

Make 5

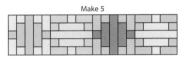

Figure 3

2. Join the rows referring to the Placement Diagram for positioning; press seams in one direction.

3. Join the K/L strips on short ends to make one long strip; press seams open. Subcut strip into two 50½" K strips and two 44½" L strips.

4. Sew a K strip to opposite long sides and L strips to the top and bottom of the pieced center; press seams toward K and L strips.

5. Join M/N strips on short ends to make one long strip; press seams open. Subcut strip into two 54½" M strips and two 56½" N strips.

6. Sew the M strips to opposite long sides and N strips to the top and bottom of the pieced center to complete the pieced top; press seams toward M and N strips.

7. Sandwich the batting between the completed top and prepared backing; pin or baste layers together to hold.

8. Quilt as desired by hand or machine; remove pins or basting. Trim excess backing and batting even with quilt top.

9. Join binding strips on short ends to make one long strip. Fold the strip in half along length with wrong sides together; press.

10. Sew binding to quilt edges, mitering corners and overlapping ends. Fold binding to the back side and stitch in place to finish. ■

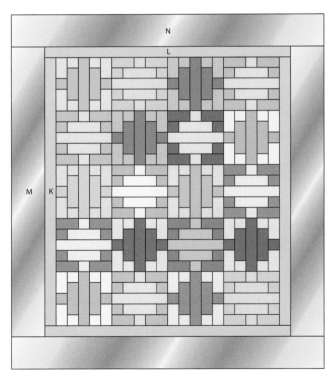

Cross Ties Throw
Placement Diagram 56" x 66"

Baby Love

Use 2½"-wide strips to piece the Heart blocks in this lovable baby quilt.

PROJECT SPECIFICATIONS

Skill Level: Beginner
Quilt Size: 36" x 44"
Block Size: 8" x 8"
Number of Blocks: 12

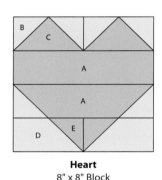

Heart
8" x 8" Block
Make 12

FABRIC Measurements based on 42" usable fabric width.	#STRIPS & PIECES	CUT
12—2½" x 42" strips pink/ yellow print	24 24 24	8½" A pieces 2½" E squares 4½" C pieces
8—2½" x 42" strips yellow/pink dot	72 24	2½" B squares 4½" D pieces
⅝ yard yellow/pink dot	4	4½" x 36½" H
¾ yard pink mottled	2 2 5	2½" x 32½" F 2½" x 28½" G 2¼" x 42" binding
Backing		42" x 50"

SUPPLIES

- Batting 42" x 50"
- Neutral color all-purpose thread
- Quilting thread
- Basic sewing tools and supplies

COMPLETING THE BLOCKS

1. Draw a diagonal line from corner to corner on the wrong side of each B and E square.

2. Place a B square on one end of C and stitch on the marked line as shown in Figure 1; trim seam to ¼" and press B to the right side, again referring to Figure 1.

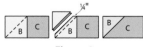

Figure 1

3. Repeat step 2 with a second B square on the opposite end of C to complete a B-C unit as shown in Figure 2. Repeat to make 24 B-C units.

Figure 2

4. Repeat step 2 with E on one end of D to complete one D-E unit as shown in Figure 3; repeat to make a reverse D-E unit, again referring to Figure 3. Repeat to make 12 each D-E and reverse D-E units.

Figure 3

5. Repeat steps 2 and 3 with B on A to complete 12 A-B units referring to Figure 4.

Figure 4

6. To complete one Heart block, join two B-C units to make a B-C row as shown in Figure 5; press seam in one direction.

Figure 5

7. Join one each D-E and reverse D-E units to complete a D-E row as shown in Figure 6.

Figure 6

8. Join the pieced rows with an A-B unit and A to complete one Heart block referring to the block drawing; press seams in one direction.

9. Repeat steps 6–8 to complete 12 Heart blocks, pressing seams of six blocks in one direction and seams in the remaining six blocks in opposite directions.

Completing the Quilt

1. Join three Heart blocks to make a row; press seams in one direction. Repeat to make four rows, pressing seams in two rows in one direction and the remaining two rows in the opposite direction.

2. Join the rows to complete the pieced center; press seams in one direction.

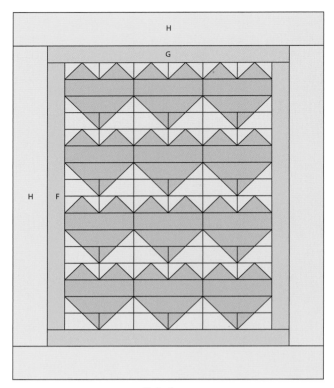

Baby Love
Placement Diagram 36" x 44"

3. Sew an F strip to opposite long sides and G strips to the top and bottom of the pieced center; press seams toward F and G strips.

4. Sew an H strip to opposite long sides and to the top and bottom of the pieced center to complete the pieced top; press seams toward the H strips.

5. Sandwich the batting between the completed top and prepared backing; pin or baste layers together to hold.

6. Quilt as desired by hand or machine; remove pins or basting. Trim excess backing and batting even with quilt top.

7. Join binding strips on short ends to make one long strip. Fold the strip in half along length with wrong sides together; press.

8. Sew binding to quilt edges, mitering corners and overlapping ends. Fold binding to the back side and stitch in place to finish. ▪

Picnic Time Quilt & Runner/Tote

A simple Rail Fence block made with a variety of 2½"-wide strips is used in the quilt and runner/tote projects.

PROJECT SPECIFICATIONS

Skill Level: Beginner
Quilt Size: 60" x 60"
Runner/Tote Size: 32" x 64"
Block Size: 8" x 8"
Number of Blocks: 36 for quilt; 21 for runner

Rail Fence
8" x 8" Block
Make 36 for quilt
Make 21 for runner/tote

FABRIC Measurements based on 42" usable fabric width.	#STRIPS & PIECES	CUT
57—2½" x 42" strips light, medium and dark prints	228	8½" A pieces
¾ yard gold print	3	4½" x 42" D
	2	4½" x 32½" E
1¼ yards red print	4	1¼" x 42" G
	4	2" x 42" F
	11	2¼" x 42" binding
1¼ yards cream print	6	6½" B/C strips
Backing		66" x 66" 38" x 70"

SUPPLIES

- Batting 66" x 66" and 38" x 70"
- Neutral color all-purpose thread
- Quilting thread
- Basic sewing tools and supplies

COMPLETING THE BLOCKS

1. Select and join four different-fabric A pieces to complete one Rail Fence block referring to the block drawing; press seams in one direction. Repeat to make 36 blocks for the quilt and 21 for the runner/tote.

COMPLETING THE QUILT

1. Join six Rail Fence blocks to make a row as shown in Figure 1; press seams in one direction. Repeat to make six rows.

Figure 1

2. Join the rows to complete the pieced center referring to the Placement Diagram for positioning; press seams in one direction.

3. Join the B/C strips on short ends to make one long strip; press seams open. Subcut the strip into two 48½" B strips and two 60½" C strips.

4. Sew B strips to opposite sides and C strips to the top and bottom of the pieced center; press seams toward B and C strips.

5. Sandwich the batting between the completed top and prepared backing; pin or baste layers together to hold.

6. Quilt as desired by hand or machine; remove pins or basting. Trim excess backing and batting even with quilt top.

7. Join binding strips on short ends to make one long strip. Fold the strip in half along length with wrong sides together; press.

8. Sew binding to quilt edges, mitering corners and overlapping ends. Fold binding to the back side and stitch in place to finish.

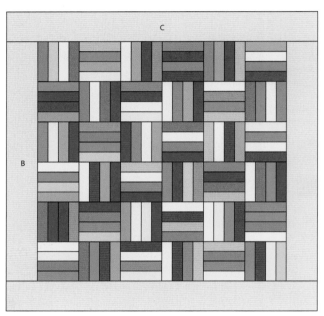

Picnic Time Quilt
Placement Diagram 60" x 60"

Completing the Runner/Tote

1. Join three Rail Fence blocks to make a row referring to Figure 2; press seams in one direction. Repeat to make seven rows.

Figure 2

2. Join the rows referring to the Placement Diagram to complete the pieced center; press seams in one direction.

3. Join the D strips on short ends to make one long strip; press seams open. Subcut into two 56½" D strips.

4. Sew a D strip to opposite long sides and E strips to the short ends of the pieced center to complete the top; press seams toward D and E strips.

5. Quilt and bind referring to steps 5–8 of Completing the Quilt.

6. Fold each long edge of each F strip ⅜" to the wrong side and press.

7. Layer two pressed F strips with wrong sides together, matching edges; stitch ¼" from each long edge to make an F handle as shown in Figure 3. Repeat to make two F handles.

Figure 3

8. Fold each end of each F strip ½" to one side; stitch to hold.

9. Measure in 5½" from the corners on each short end of the runner/tote and mark with a pin as shown in Figure 4.

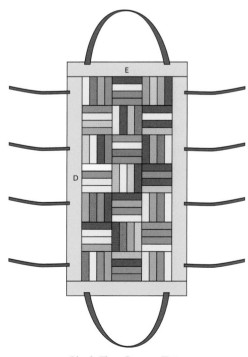

Picnic Time Runner/Tote
Placement Diagram 32" x 64"

Figure 4

10. Pin an F strip 1½" down from the top edge with one edge aligned with the inside edge of the pin as shown in Figure 5; stitch a square shape in the strip end to secure. Repeat with the opposite end of the strip at the other corner of the runner/tote to complete the handle, again referring to Figure 5.

Figure 5

11. Repeat step 10 with second F strip on the opposite short end of the runner/tote.

12. Fold each long edge of each G strip to the wrong side ¼" and press.

13. Fold one pressed edge over the other to enclose raw edges and stitch to hold as shown in Figure 6; cut each stitched strip in half at an angle to make eight tie strips. Stitch across the angled raw ends.

Figure 6

14. Fold the straight end of each strip to the wrong side ½"; stitch to hold.

15. Measure and place a pin 8" from each end and 15" apart on each long side of the runner/tote as shown in Figure 7.

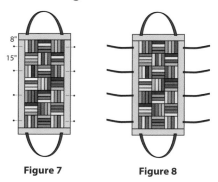

Figure 7   **Figure 8**

16. Align, pin and stitch a tie strip even with each pin referring to Figure 8 to complete the runner/tote. ■

Credits

Bric-a-Brac Quilt page 1: Various strips from Troy Riverwoods collections by Kathy Brown of The Teacher's Pet.

Road Block Quilt page 5: Moda's Cranberry Wishes Jelly Roll by Lynn Hagemier of Kansas Troubles Quilters.

Cross Ties Throw page 7: Moda's Dandelion Girl Jelly Roll by Joanna Figueroa of Fig Tree Quilts.

Baby Love Blanket page 10: Troy Riverwoods Cat Nap'n fabric collection by Kathy Brown of The Teacher's Pet.

Picnic Time Quilt & Runner/Tote page 13: Moda's Summer Basket of Flowers Jelly Roll by Terry Clothier Thompson.

Quilts pieced by Kathy Brown of The Teacher's Pet, Linda Reed and Antonia Cangemi.

Quilts quilted on a longarm machine by Kathy Brown of The Teacher's Pet, Ellen Rushin of Seven Stitches Machine Quilting with additional help from Cheryl Wilks.

E-mail: Customer_Service@DRGnetwork.com

HOUSE of WHITE BIRCHES PUBLISHERS SINCE 1947

Jelly Roll Quilts is published by DRG, 306 East Parr Road, Berne, IN 46711, telephone (260) 589-4000. Printed in USA.

RETAIL STORES: If you would like to carry this pattern book or any other DRG publications, call the Wholesale Department at Annie's Attic to set up a direct account: (903) 636-4303. Also, request a complete listing of publications available from DRG.

Every effort has been made to ensure that the instructions in this pattern book are complete and accurate. We cannot, however, take responsibility for human error, typographical mistakes or variations in individual work.

ISBN: 978-1-59217-237-5
3 4 5 6 7 8 9

STAFF
Editors: Jeanne Stauffer, Sandra L. Hatch
Managing Editor: Dianne Schmidt
Technical Artist: Connie Rand
Copy Supervisor: Michelle Beck
Copy Editors: Sue Harvey, Judy Weatherford, Renee Wright

Graphic Arts Supervisor: Ronda Bechinski
Graphic Artists: Erin Augsburger, Joanne Gonzalez
Art Director: Brad Snow
Assistant Art Director: Nick Pierce
Photography Supervisor: Tammy Christian
Photography: Matthew Owen
Photo Stylist: Tammy Steiner